PIONEERS OF SCIENCE

LEONARDO DA VINCI

Peter Lafferty

Pioneers of Science

Alexander Graham Bell
Marie Curie
Michael Faraday
Leonardo da Vinci
Guglielmo Marconi
Isaac Newton

Series editor: Rosemary Ashley
Designer: David Armitage

First published in 1990 by
Wayland (Publishers) Limited
61 Western Road, Hove
East Sussex BN3 1JD, England

© 1990 Wayland (Publishers) Limited

British Library Cataloguing in Publication Data
Lafferty, Peter
   Leonardo da Vinci
   1. Science. Theories of Leonardo, da Vinci, 1452–1519
   I. Title
   509'.2'4

   ISBN 1–85210–870–3

Typeset by Nicola Taylor, Wayland
Printed in Italy by Rotolito Lombarda S.p.A
Bound in France by A.G.M.

Contents

1 Leonardo's World   4
2 Early Life in Florence   7
3 The Emerging Scientist   14
4 Leonardo's Science   22
5 The Years of Wandering   28
6 Rome – City of Disappointment   37
7 The Final Years   42
Date Chart   46
Books to Read   46
Glossary   47
Index   48

1 ▼ Leonardo's World

Leonardo da Vinci was born near Florence, in Italy, about 500 years ago. It was a time of rapid change. In many ways, the changes going on in Italy at that time were like those affecting us today. Leonardo's world was being expanded by the opening up of new lands by Columbus and other explorers, just as space exploration is extending our knowledge of other worlds today. The new, explosive power of gunpowder was being used in war for the first time, just as the power of nuclear weapons has been used for the first time in this century. The appearance of the first printed books in Leonardo's time made communication between large numbers of people easy; radio and television have made a similar impact in modern times.

Changes like these affect the way that people think. In Leonardo's day, as in ours, there was unrest. Accepted views on religion, politics, art and science were being challenged. During this time, the ideas of the great thinkers of Ancient Greece were rediscovered in Europe. The period became known as the 'Renaissance', or the 'rebirth'.

Italy was not then a single country as it is today. It consisted of five great city states, Milan, Venice, Florence, Rome and Naples. The rulers of these states were not elected by the people. They were dictators and relied on hired soldiers, bribery and corruption to get their own way. At the same time, to show off their success and fame they encouraged the arts of painting, sculpture and architecture. Each ruler surrounded himself with artists to paint pictures of him, architects to build monuments to glorify his achievements and scholars to write about him and his exploits. The same artists and architects also served their masters as military engineers, for this was a time of war in Italy.

Artist inventors like Leonardo were in great demand as military engineers during the sixteenth century. This is one of Leonardo's many designs for improved weapons of war.

Columbus lands in San Salvador, in what is now the Bahamas, in 1492.

The ruler of Florence at the time of Leonardo's birth was Cosimo de' Medici. He was one of the richest men in Europe, having made money from the wool trade and banking. During his rule, there was a steady flow into Italy of immigrants from Constantinople (now called Istanbul). These refugees spoke Greek and brought with them many precious Greek manuscripts. Cosimo set up a school, or 'Academy', under a learned scholar, Marsilio Ficino, who was an expert on the ideas of Plato, the great Greek thinker. Cosimo's grandson, Lorenzo, carried on developing Florence with such success that he came to be called, 'Il Magnifico', 'the Magnificent'.

Under the rule of the Medici family Florence produced many gifted citizens. The Florentines thought that a person should have a wide range of skills and interests. A person should be 'whole and complete', and not limited in outlook by religion or profession.

Foremost among the citizens of Florence was Leonardo da Vinci, the most brilliant artist the city had ever seen. He was also an architect, a musician, a scientist, a mathematician and an inventor of genius. More than any other person Leonardo fulfilled the Renaissance ideal of the 'whole and complete' person for he excelled in both science and art.

5

As a scientist, Leonardo was the first to see clearly that knowledge about the world must be based on experiments, and not on untested ideas. He also knew that mathematics was an important tool for the scientist. He failed in many of his scientific investigations only because there were no accurate instruments to use in his experiments, and the mathematics needed in science had not been discovered. Later scientists, such as Galileo and Newton, had better tools and made more important discoveries, but Leonardo is still remembered as a true pioneer of science and technology.

2 Early Life in Florence

Leonardo was born on 15 April 1452, in the village of Vinci. The village lies high up on Mount Albano, which stands in the valley of the River Arno near the city of Florence. Leonardo's mother, Caterina, was an unmarried peasant girl. His father, Piero da Vinci was the son of a Florentine lawyer. After Leonardo's birth, Piero was quickly persuaded to marry into a wealthy family. Caterina was married off to a cowherd.

Leonardo at first lived with his father's parents. However, after a few years, Piero realized that his wife could have no children. So he took Leonardo, who was an attractive and promising boy, into his family.

Leonardo was a bright child. He was quick at arithmetic and music. He learned to play the lyre, a popular musical instrument of the time, and could sing beautifully. He also showed promise at drawing, sketching the plants and animals he saw around him on Mount Albano.

Florence at the time of Leonardo. Verrocchio's studio, where Leonardo developed his artistic skills, was near to the large tower in the centre of the picture.

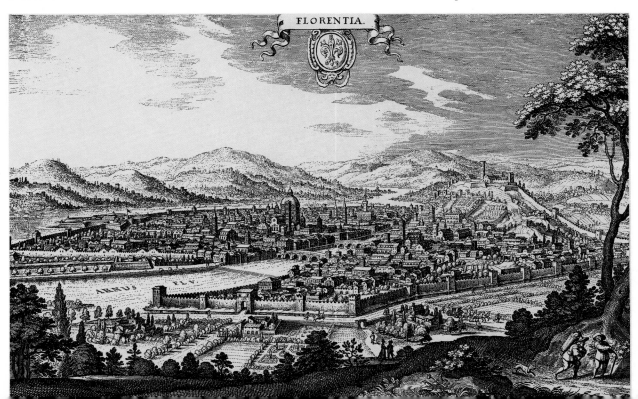

A drawing by Leonardo of rock formations which he saw in the countryside near Florence. Geology was just one of the many subjects he studied.

   In 1469, Leonardo was sent to work with an artist called Verrocchio in his workshop in Florence. Verrocchio was a man of all-round ability. He was a skilled craftsman, a goldsmith, a sculptor and painter, and from him Leonardo learned all these skills.

Leonardo and Verrocchio explored two fields of knowledge to help them with their artistic work, human anatomy and perspective. Anatomy is the study of the structure of the body, and is usually learned by cutting up, or dissecting, bodies. Perspective is the study of how solid, three-dimensional objects can be drawn on a flat, two-dimensional surface, such as a sheet of paper, so that the drawing shows accurately how the object looks.

During his time with Verrocchio, Leonardo's interests broadened. Wandering along the banks of the River Arno and in the countryside around Florence, his observant eye began to note rock formations, caves and fossils. What he saw in the layers of rock and their fossils raised questions in his mind. It was the same

Observation and drawing of plants and flowers were to be important in Leonardo's development as a scientist.

with the plants he saw. Here in the Arno valley, he began his detailed study of plants. The results of these can be seen in his paintings of flowers and trees.

In 1476, misfortune overtook Leonardo. For the whole of his life, he never seemed very interested in women, except as mother figures. This suggested to some people that he was a homosexual. A charge was brought against him and others by an unknown person who wrote an unsigned letter to the city governors. The charge was dismissed, but it caused Leonardo much distress.

Leonardo's mental powers may have set him apart from others and made him lonely, for throughout his life he seems to have had very few close friends. Yet his kindness and sympathy were noticed by many. He was very fond of horses and trained them with great kindness and patience. Some stories say that when he passed markets where birds were sold, he would buy the birds and let them out of their cages. This love of animals made him a vegetarian. It also hindered his search for knowledge, for he hardly ever performed experiments on animals.

In about 1477, Leonardo left Verrocchio's studio to make his own independent career. His remaining years in Florence were not happy. His life was scarred by the accusation of homosexuality. Although he worked for a time for Lorenzo de' Medici as a sculptor, he did not mix with the other scholars of Florence.

During the years spent in Verrocchio's studio, Leonardo found that he was good at inventing machines. He delighted in what we would call the technology of his day. It was part of his defence against the scholars of Florence to say that, 'They go about puffed up and pompous, in fine raiment and bejewelled, not from the fruits of their own labour but from those of others. My work they refuse to recognize. They despise me the inventor, but how much more are they to blame for not being inventors, but trumpeters and reciters of the works of others?'

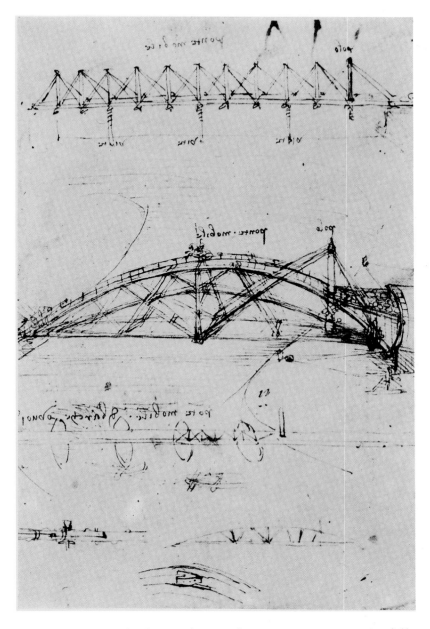

Leonardo's claim to be an inventor was not an idle boast. In about 1481, he wrote a letter to the Duke of Milan, Ludovico Sforza, asking for employment. He wrote,

'I can construct bridges very light and strong, capable of easy transportation, and with them you may pursue and on occasion flee from the enemy; and still others capable of resisting fire and attack, easy and convenient to place and remove; and methods of burning and destroying those of the enemy.

When a place is besieged I know how to remove the water from the moats, and make an infinite number of bridges, covered ways, ladders and other instruments suitable to the said purposes.

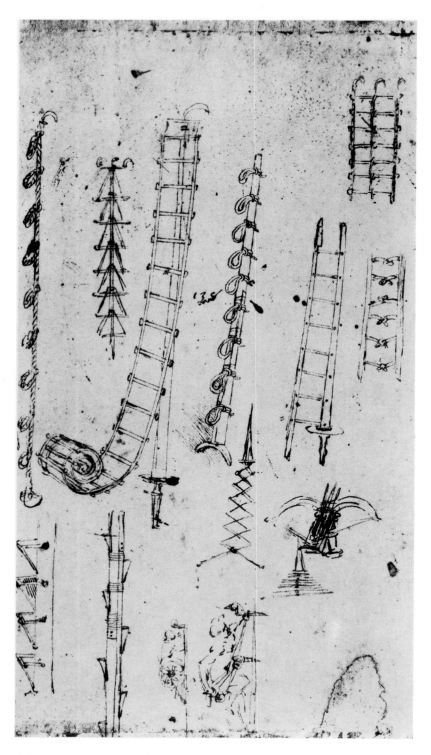

Drawings of different types of ladders for climbing castle walls.

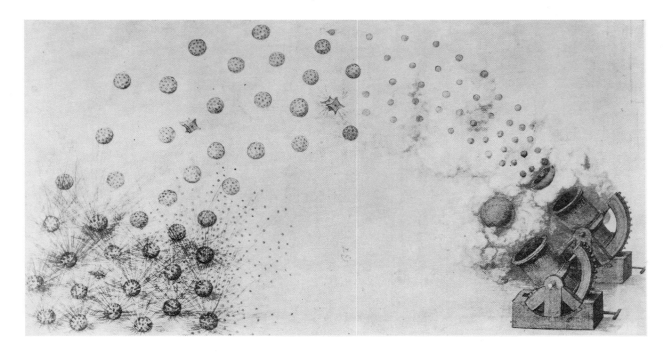

I have also plans of mortars most convenient and easy to carry, with which to hurl small stones similar to a storm, and with their smoke cause great terror to the enemy and great damage and confusion.

And if it should happen that the fight were at sea I have plans for many instruments capable of offence and defence, and vessels which will resist the fire of the largest cannon, powder and smoke.

Also I will make covered cars, safe and unassailable which will enter among the enemy with their artillery and break up the largest body of men.'

Leonardo's design for an early cannon, with exploding cannonballs.

One of the most astonishing things about this letter is that drawings for all of these claims can be found in Leonardo's notebooks. Only as an afterthought did Leonardo mention that he was also an artist,

'Also I can carry out sculpture in marble, bronze or clay; similarly in painting I can do whatever can be done as well as any other whoever he may be.'

After such a magnificent letter of application, it seems odd that Leonardo was invited to Milan with great ceremony by Ludovico 'to play the lyre in which the duke greatly delighted.'

3 ▼ The Emerging Scientist

When Leonardo went to Milan in 1482, he was already accepted as a master painter and highly thought of as an inventor. It was as an artist-engineer that Leonardo was to get jobs for the rest of his life. What was not recognized was that he was making painting and engineering into a science.

Leonardo's development from technologist to scientist took place during twenty years of hard struggle. Although he began his working career as more of an artist than a scientist, Leonardo finished his life as more of a scientist than an artist.

For some years after he went to Milan, Leonardo was frustrated. As a 'foreigner', he found it difficult to obtain work. Eventually, he was offered a contract to paint a religious picture for a group of monks. He produced a masterpiece, called *The Virgin of the Rocks*. It was far richer in design, colour and feeling than the monks had expected. They accused Leonardo of not doing what they asked and took him to court. The argument went on for over twenty years.

The picture showed how Leonardo had progressed in his studies of light, shade and perspective. Leonardo explained that the shapes of objects are not made up of lines but differences in light and shade. Leonardo was able to paint these differences and produce the appearance of real objects.

In his early years in Florence and Milan, Leonardo produced a great number of inventions. Although he never stopped inventing until his death, it was during this period of his life that he invented most.

Leonardo spent a lot of time gun-making and inventing flying machines. Guns interested him, not so much for their military use, but because they enabled him to study how objects moved at high speeds. He

Right *The Virgin of the Rocks* did not please the monks who commissioned it, but it is now considered a masterpiece.

14

Scientific study of flight

It was only after his early failure that Leonardo came to realize the many factors involved in human flight. After some years without success, he set about studying birds' bodies. Systematically, he worked out the distribution of their weight and measured the span and area of their wings in relation to their weight. He even calculated the amount of muscle a person would need to be able to flap 'wings' and fly. When he realized the importance of a bird's tail for balancing and steering, he studied models of them and the effects air currents had on them.

He then observed how a large bird often flies without beating its wings. 'The wind which passes under the wing lifts it up just as a wedge lifts a weight,' he wrote. He gave as an example, 'the flight of cranes...which proceed to raise themselves by many turns after the manner of a screw...and a screw is of the nature of a wedge' (note his drawing below). But this observation came too late in his life for him to turn it into a practical invention.

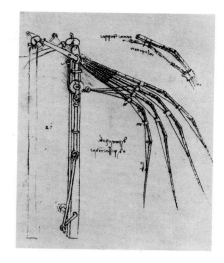

Leonardo's design for the wing of a flying machine.

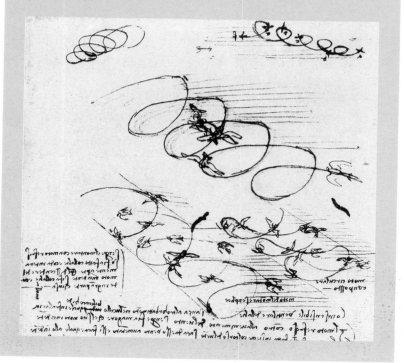

invented multi-barrelled guns and a steam-powered gun. He also studied the action of gunpowder.

Leonardo's work on flying machines came from a desire to imitate bird flight. All his early efforts used flapping wings. Later, he used the principle of the propeller, the helicopter, and finally that of the hot-air balloon. Leonardo's attempts to achieve human flight show a gradual change from trial-and-error methods to a scientific approach.

The first successful helicopter was designed in the 1930's, on principles studied by Leonardo over four hundred years earlier.

He also experimented with the use of water power. Many of his drawings of water-wheels show them powering machines such as mills, and bellows for furnaces. He drew up detailed and ambitious plans for building canals to transport goods and for irrigation. He put these plans into practice in a canal system around Milan.

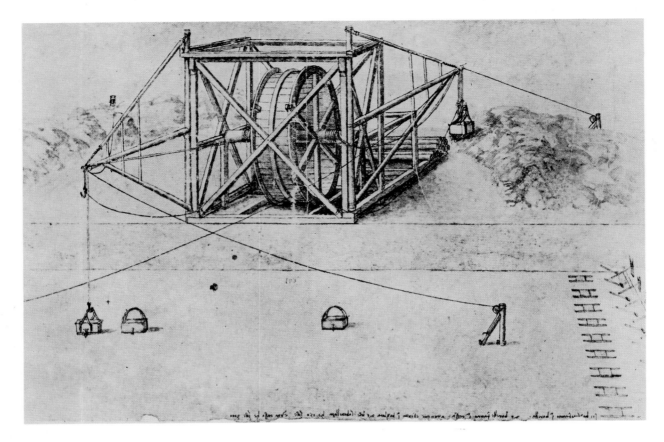

A drawing of machinery for excavating canals.

Leonardo's notes for this period contain many architectural plans for cathedrals. It is typical of Leonardo that his experiments in architecture began with a study of building tools and instruments. He also studied the strength of beams, pillars and arches. Such studies of the strengths of materials had never been made before.

Leonardo briefly went back to his work on anatomy. This was partly due to his interest in the similarities he saw between buildings and the human body, but also because he wanted to continue his study of perspective. His experiments had shown him that there were marked differences in size and shape of the 'real object' and its image as seen by the eye. How did this come about? Was the Greek thinker, Plato, right when he said that we cannot trust our senses? In the rules of perspective, Leonardo found part of the answer, but he had to go on and study the structure of the eye and its connection to the brain.

Early inventions

Some of Leonardo's earliest inventions related to his studies of light and vision. A machine for lens-grinding and polishing appeared as early as 1478. He devised methods for raising water using twisting screws at about this time too. One of his simplest and most ingenious inventions was his turn-spit for roasting meat. This was controlled by the current of heated air rising from the fire (see below). In the workshop itself, Leonardo gave a lot of thought to the tools he used and was continually trying to improve his equipment. To this end, he invented file-making machines, mechanical saws, machines for boring holes, and lifting devices.

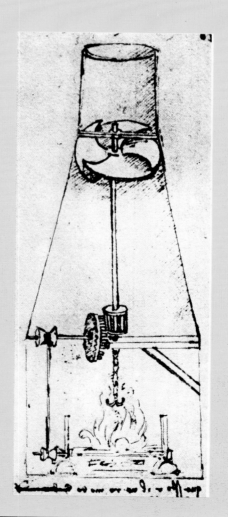

Below Water raising devices using the scientific principle of the screw.

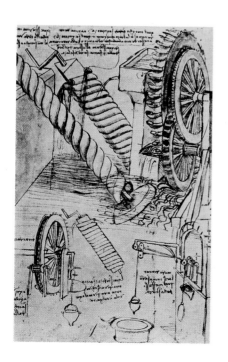

In 1489, he began a new notebook on human anatomy. It contains crude sketches of the eye, and of the optic nerve entering an equally crudely sketched brain. Apart from some splendid drawings of the socket of the eye and the skull, these early drawings did little more than open the doors of a vast new world for Leonardo. But he was not ready to explore this new world yet, not until he had made more progress in discovering the 'rules' of physics which describe how the world works. For nearly twenty years he abandoned his human anatomical research.

In 1495, Leonardo began work on a painting called *The Last Supper* on the wall of the dining hall of the monastery attached to Santa Maria della Grazie – Duke Ludovico's favourite church. This was to be one of his greatest masterpieces. Unfortunately, the materials he used were of poor quality, and the painting soon began to crumble and fade.

A scale model of Leonardo's flying machine constructed for an exhibition in 1988. It was made by following Leonardo's drawings and the same materials as he specified: beech wood, wax, brass, rope, leather and tallow. The wings were to be covered with light cloth.

The Last Supper, *Leonardo's masterpiece depicting Jesus and his disciples.*

During his last years under Duke Ludovico in Milan, Leonardo made friends with a mathematician called Luca Pacioli. This man taught Leonardo about geometry and arithmetic. It was through Pacioli that Leonardo came to value mathematics, especially geometry, so highly. He came to see geometry behind all Nature. He wrote, 'Let no man who is not a mathematician read the elements of my works,' and, 'There is no certainty where one cannot apply any of the mathematical sciences.' Today, every scientist would think this obvious, but in Leonardo's day this was an important new idea.

In 1499, after Duke Ludovico had been defeated in battle by the French, Leonardo left Milan with his friend, Luca Pacioli.

4 Leonardo's Science

Before we can understand how Leonardo tried to build his knowledge into a science, we need first to picture the differences between the world that Leonardo lived in and the world that we live in today. Leonardo was a citizen of the fifteenth century. He would have been amazed at the knowledge possessed by even a small child today. To him, television, computers and nuclear bombs would be beyond belief. Aeroplanes, a product of the twentieth century, would remind him that he failed to make one. Power from a petrol engine or steam turbine he would easily understand. However, he would be completely dazed when told that water consisted of two elements, hydrogen and oxygen. To him, the 'elements' were earth, fire, air and water. That is what the word 'element' meant in Leonardo's time, and would continue to mean for another three hundred years.

In about 1490, Leonardo's notes changed from being mainly descriptions of inventions, to being a record of his search for the principles underlying those inventions. He began to look for what he called 'rules'. He discussed ways of obtaining knowledge. He argued about the value of careful observation and experiment. He was changing from an artist-inventor into a scientist.

In Leonardo's time, the study of religion was called 'the queen of the sciences'. True knowledge, it was thought, came only from studying the Bible. Knowledge gained through experience was said to be full of error and mostly worthless. Leonardo disagreed with this idea. He said, 'All knowledge has its origins in our senses.' And, because the sense most capable of bringing true knowledge is vision, Leonardo wrote, 'The eye, the window of the soul, is the chief means

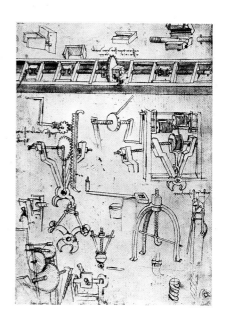

A typical page from an early notebook, crammed with ideas for new machines and tools. Later notebooks show more of Leonardo's search for scientific knowledge and understanding through experiment and observation.

whereby the understanding can most fully and abundantly appreciate the infinite works of Nature; and the ear is second.'

But, at the same time, Leonardo was well aware that the eye can be tricked. He had carried out many experiments on perspective. With these he sorted out the causes of false appearances, or optical illusions. These experiments had made clear to him the conditions in which the true proportions of objects can be seen – and then reproduced by the painter. 'The eye,' he wrote, 'sees only by straight lines which compose a pyramid which forms the base of the object and conducts it to the eye.'

Leonardo felt that through his work on perspective he had discovered and proved a basic law about light. Its power gets progressively weaker as it travels in circles outwards from a shining object. This was an entirely new theory of light. It was to be almost two hundred years before the theory was fully accepted by other scientists.

Leonardo believed that the wave-movements in water were the same as those that took place in air, with light and with sound. 'Although voices penetrating the air spread in circular movements from their causes, none the less the circles move from different centres, meet and penetrate and pass one another without impediment, always keeping to their causal centres.

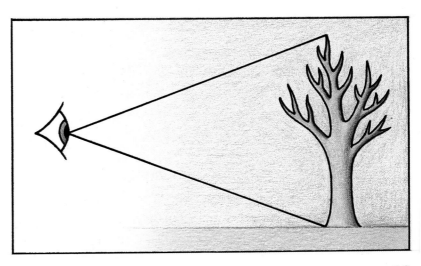

According to Leonardo, light travelled from an object to the eye in straight lines, forming a pyramid, or triangle.

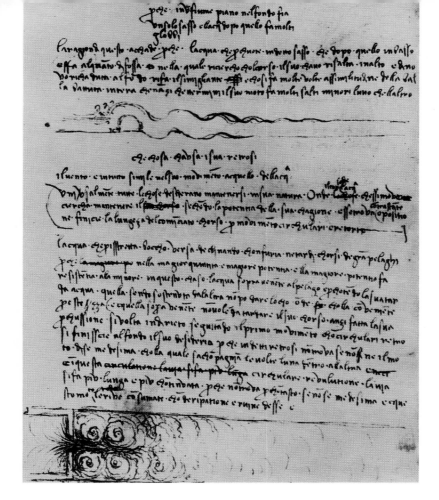

Because in all instances of movements there is great similarity between water and air.'

Leonardo used his wave theory of forces in space to explain all other forms of power or energy known to him, such as sound and heat and even the power of a magnet. All these forces, said Leonardo, lessened 'pyramidally' from their sources as they spread outwards in circles.

Just as Leonardo accepted that there were four elements, earth, air, fire and water, he also accepted the ideas of the Ancient Greek thinker Aristotle about the way forces move objects. Aristotle had said that, except for 'natural' movements such as falling, all movements needed a mover or force. Leonardo decided that 'percussion' was such a force and that it was more important and greater than any of the other forces generated in the four elements of Nature, because, 'Percussion in equal time exceeds any other power.'

Experiments on movement

Leonardo found evidence for his ideas from his experiments on the movement of water.

He observed that, 'If you throw a stone into the water it becomes the centre and cause of many circles...' and, 'If you throw two stones at the same time on to a sheet of motionless water at some distance from one another, you will see that around the two percussions two quantities of separate circles are caused, which as they increase in size will meet and then penetrate and intersect one another, whilst all the time maintaining as their respective centres the places percussed by the stones.'

Leonardo used the word 'percussion' to mean a blow or impulse.

It concentrates greatest force into least time. His many experiments into the connection between forces and the movements they produced led him to such rules as, 'Percussion is greatest along its central line.' You can demonstrate this rule by throwing a tennis ball at a wall. The ball will hit the wall more powerfully when it is thrown straight at it, 'along its central line.' Another rule, 'The angle of incidence of percussion always equals the angle of reflection', Leonardo applied not only to light and cannon balls, but to the movements of water in rivers, and of blood in the heart.

A further force that was not in Aristotle's world of physics is one called 'impetus.' Leonardo defined it as, 'a power impressed by the mover on the moved thing.'

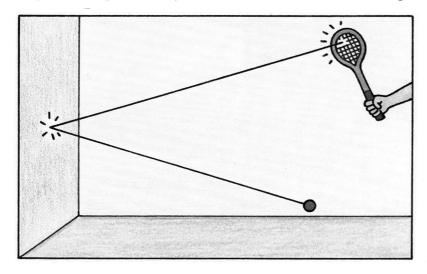

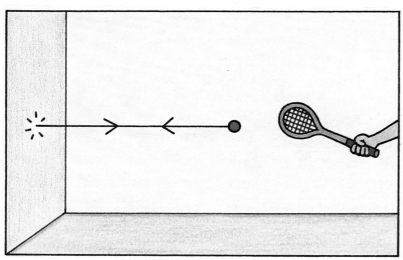

A ball will hit a wall more powerfully straight on than at an angle. This demonstrates Leonardo's rule that, 'Percussion is greatest along its central line'.

Leonardo invented the bicycle 300 years before it appeared on the road. Modern bicycles use Leonardo's invention of ball-bearings to reduce friction in their moving parts.

At the same time, he made many studies of friction. Friction causes a moving object to lose power and Leonardo measured how much power is lost when an object moves across a rough surface. His work on friction led him to invent ball-bearings to reduce friction in his machines.

Since he believed that there was no movement in Nature which did not meet with resistance or friction, Leonardo did not reach Newton's idea of inertia. Newton's idea was that every body continues in a state of rest or uniform motion in a straight line unless made to change that state. For Leonardo, all 'impetus' gradually came to an end 'pyramidally'. He did, however, state repeatedly that in all the elements 'action equals reaction' and 'the movement of air against a fixed thing equals the movement of a moved thing against immovable air.' And it is the same in water, for example, 'movement of water against an oar equals the movement of the oar against water.' This anticipated Newton's third law which states that to every action there is an equal and opposite reaction.

5 ▽ The Years of Wandering

After his long stay of eighteen years in Milan, Leonardo became a wanderer. First, he went to Venice. At the time, the Turks were attacking Venice. The worried citizens asked Leonardo for his advice on their defences. Leonardo gave them a plan for flooding the River Isonzo on their frontier. He also designed a diving suit which would allow divers to bore holes in enemy ships and sink them. Then he left for Florence.

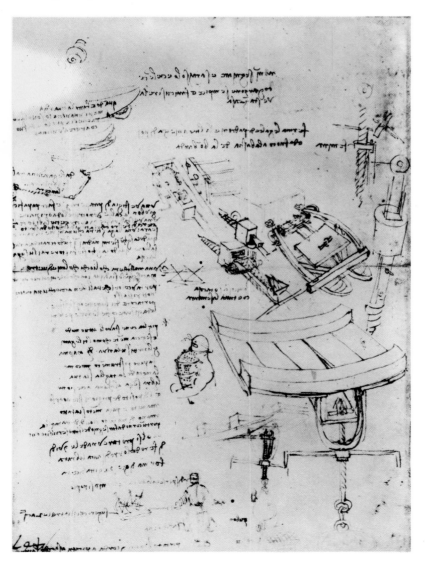

To the left of this device for sinking ships is a small sketch of a diving suit with goggles. The front of the suit holds a 'wineskin containing air' for breathing — an early form of the aqualung.

In 1501, back in his native city, he was asked to paint an altar-piece for a monastery. The cartoon, or preliminary drawing, which he did of the painting filled everyone with wonder. It was called *The Virgin and St Anne with the Christ Child.*

The next year, Leonardo was asked to act as engineer with the army of Cesare Borgia, the Pope's military commander, who was attempting to gain control of central Italy by force. It is surprising that Leonardo should join Cesare Borgia. He was probably attracted by the chance to put his new theories into practice. The notebook, which Leonardo kept during the next eight months, does not mention the military campaign. Instead there are notes on the flight of birds, the drainage of marshes, bridge-building, the formation of waves and ideas for making maps. He drew the first scale maps from his travels across Italy. This led him to study the formation of the Earth. He was the first to recognize that fossils are the remains of long-dead life forms. He denounced the biblical story of the Flood. He then produced a theory that the Earth had grown out of the waters which ages ago had covered it.

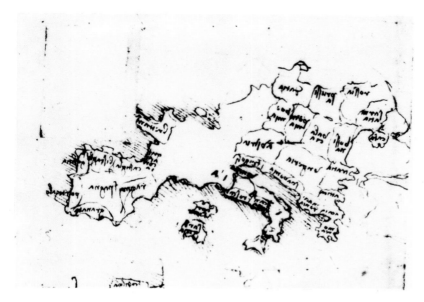

Although Leonardo's comments on Cesare Borgia's wars are not found in his notebooks, he painted them on the walls of the Palazzo Vecchio in Florence in 1504. The painting was called *The Battle of Anghiari*. Unfortunately, the painting was destroyed when Leonardo tried an experimental method of drying it by fire. Only one copy of this picture has survived, but this is enough to show Leonardo's thoughts about war. It is a painting showing the great violence and cruelty of war most clearly. Since Leonardo had also failed in his latest attempt to get his flying machine off the ground, Florence was once more a city of disappointment for him. He could not bring himself to begin the painting all over again, even though this was demanded of him. When, in 1506, King Louis XII of France asked him to go back to Milan, Leonardo went willingly, with great relief.

Leonardo was about to do some of the most brilliant research of his life. By now, he had built up a theory of how the 'four powers' – movement, weight, force and percussion – worked in the world at large. He was now ready to use the theory to understand the small world of the human body. In about 1508, he set about investigating the various parts of the human body and how they worked.

Right The Virgin and St Anne with the Christ Child, *completed while Leonardo was back in his native city.*

To accomplish his plan, Leonardo had to dissect about thirty corpses. As he dissected and drew, Leonardo was repeatedly overcome with the beauty and wonder of what he was revealing. His notebooks are scattered with exclamations of admiration. For example, beside a figure of the heart he exclaimed, 'Marvellous instrument invented by the Supreme Master!'

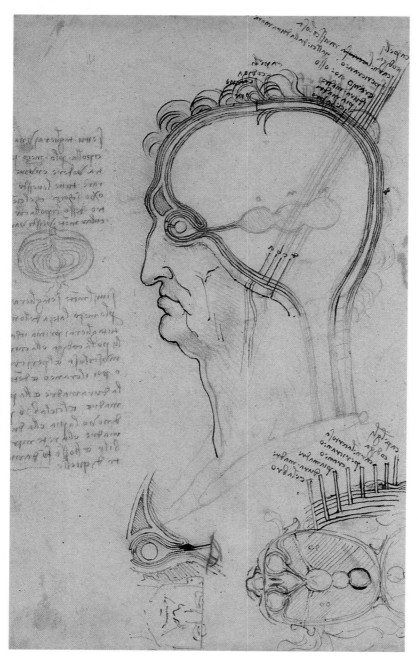

An early sketch of a human skull. Leonardo made this drawing before he carried out dissections of the human body.

Research into anatomy

In order to discover the true shapes of cavities like those inside the brain and heart, Leonardo used his experience as a sculptor. He injected these organs with wax and made plaster casts. His drawings of the skeleton showed his knowledge of the movements and postures of the body. It was Leonardo who showed for the first time the true shape of the spine and the tilt of the pelvis.

The arms and legs gave him a good chance to explain his principles of the lever. Every muscle was dissected to show how it acted to make the bony levers work. Having dissected out a muscle, Leonardo would tug it to show how it worked. In this way, he built up a complete picture of how the limbs and their joints moved. One which really pleased him was the action of the biceps, a muscle in the upper arm. This muscle, he found, not only bent the arm at the elbow but turned the palm of the hand upwards as well. He made a number of drawings to show how it did this.

When he had worked out how all the muscles in the leg worked, he made a model, putting onto its bones copper wires which ran along what he called the 'lines of force' of each muscle.

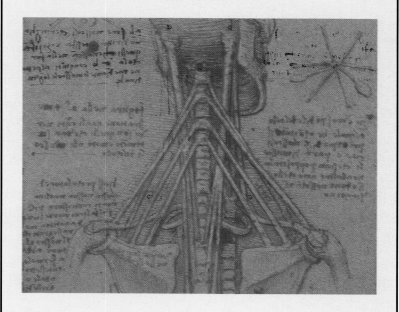

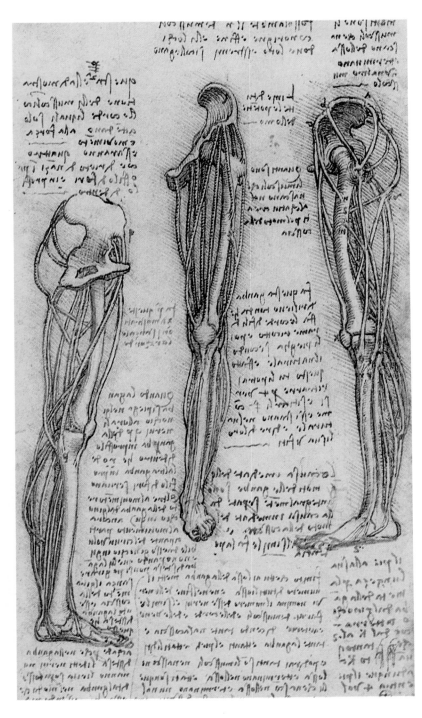

Leonardo's drawings of an infant before it is born are probably the most famous of his anatomical drawings. He also made beautiful drawings of the main organs inside a woman's body. At about the same time, he was painting his most famous painting, the *Mona Lisa*, a portrait of the wife of a citizen of Florence.

Right Leonardo's drawing of an unborn child in the womb.

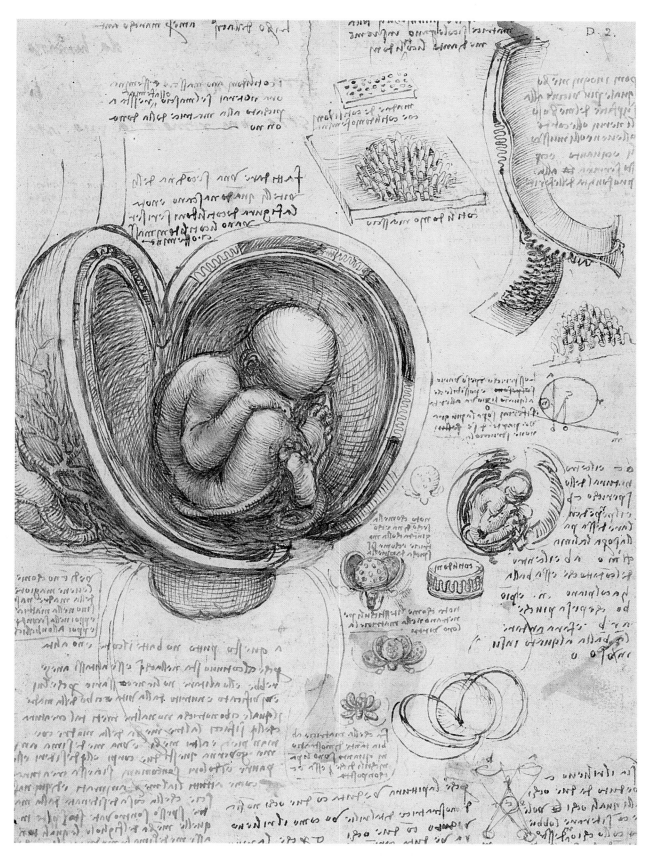

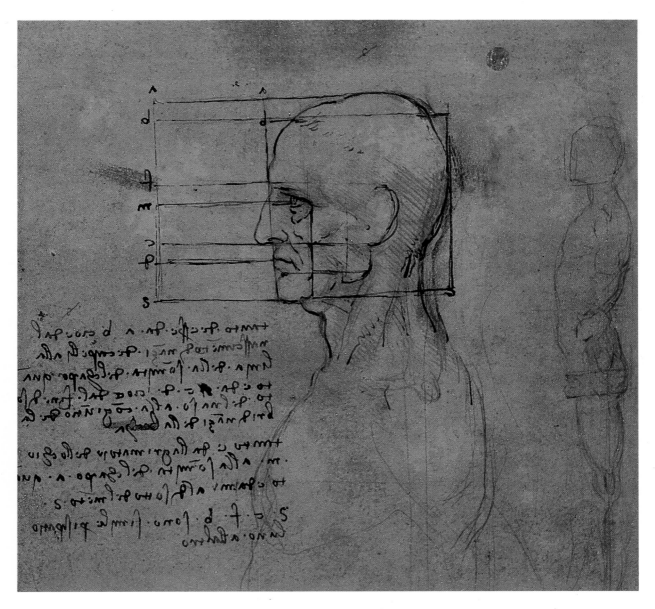

A study of the proportions of the human head.

Most of his anatomical work was done in Milan, or in Florence when he briefly visited his home town. For a while he lived a peaceful life. However, these short years of peace were soon to end. In April 1512, the French were driven from Milan. Young Maximilian, son of Ludovico Sforza, returned to the city. Leonardo, having served the French, was no longer welcome. But in the meantime, Pope Julius II had been succeeded in Rome by Pope Leo X, the son of Leonardo's earliest patron, Lorenzo de' Medici. So, on 24 September 1513, Leonardo left Milan for Rome.

6 Rome – City of Disappointment

Leonardo arrived in Rome full of hope. Pope Leo, together with his brother Giuliano de' Medici, promised to turn Rome into a bigger and better Florence. Pope Leo was a typical Renaissance figure – learned, cultured and fond of the arts, particularly music. Unfortunately, Leo was scornful of mechanical experiments, but Giuliano was different. He sensed the mystery and importance of science. His interest was alchemy, a partly scientific form of chemistry which was mainly devoted to trying to turn common metals into gold. Giuliano saw to it that Leonardo was well paid and lodged in luxurious quarters in the palace of Belvedere, on the top of the Vatican hill. Leonardo was provided with a laboratory and a workshop with paid assistants. At last Leonardo had the ideal place for his work.

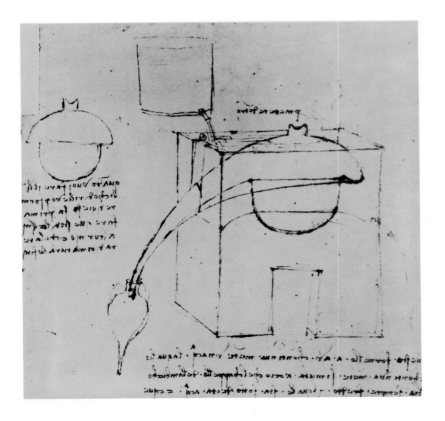

Leonardo's genius served him in the laboratory, too. This retort, or bottle, for distilling, is kept cool by cold water which pours from the vessel on the left.

Leonardo had no belief in alchemy, but because of Giuliano's interests, he began to look at the subjects in his own way. When, in the past, he had made his own paints, he had made improved distilling flasks which could be cooled down more easily. He used these in his laboratory in Rome with substances he called Venus, Mercury and Jupiter – the alchemist's names for copper, mercury and tin.

When it came to the preparation of improved varnish for his paintings, his experiments failed. Pope Leo thought this very amusing. Here was Leonardo busy preparing the varnish before he had even begun to paint a picture. 'Alas,' he exclaimed, 'this man will never get anything done, for he is thinking about the end before he begins.' This spiteful comment shows the different

A model of Leonardo's screw-cutting machine. Leonardo's own machine was still in use up until the twentieth century.

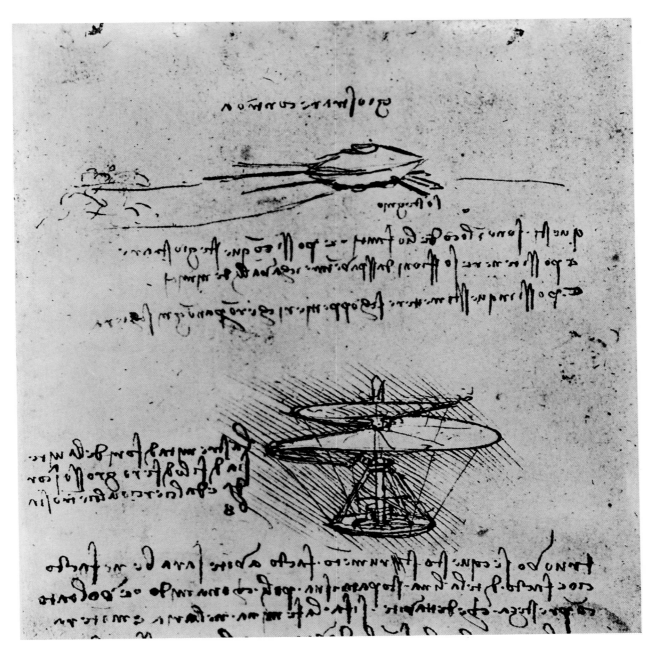

thinking of the two men. It also explains why the Pope gave very little work to Leonardo while he was in Rome.

In his laboratory, Leonardo turned to the invention of metal screws which, until then, had never been used. He produced a screw-cutting machine which was in use up to the twentieth century. This machine was the result of his many studies of the screw which had been part of his work on the helicopter and propeller.

A sketch for a helicopter based on Leonardo's scientific study of the action of the screw. Igor Sikorsky, who perfected the helicopter in the 1940's, is said to have been inspired by a book about Leonardo's inventions given to him as a child.

39

Study of the heart

Leonardo also began to study the anatomy of the heart very carefully, using hearts of cattle from the slaughter-house. His studies led him to disagree completely with the old ideas about what the heart was and how it worked. These ideas came from Aristotle and the Greek doctor, Galen, who lived in the 2nd century AD. Galen thought the heart was a centre of the life force, or 'vital spirit', and emotional feeling. The heart heated the blood which then flowed out through the blood vessels, called arteries, with the 'vital spirit'. The heart was thought to be too 'noble' to be just a muscle.

Leonardo felt that there was a great deal wrong with these ideas. In the slaughter-house, he watched pigs being killed by having skewers thrust into their heart. There he saw the movements of the dying pigs' hearts. He noticed that the beat of the heart coincided with the movement of blood into the main arteries. He was very interested in the way blood flowed into and out of the heart and made a glass model of the heart so that he could examine it more closely. The heart, he saw, was just a muscle that pumped blood around the body. He made many detailed drawings of the heart and the blood vessels connected to it.

During the years in Rome, Leonardo's health began to fail. We know this from a letter he wrote to Giuliano de' Medici, who was himself seriously ill with tuberculosis. Leonardo wrote, 'So greatly did I rejoice,

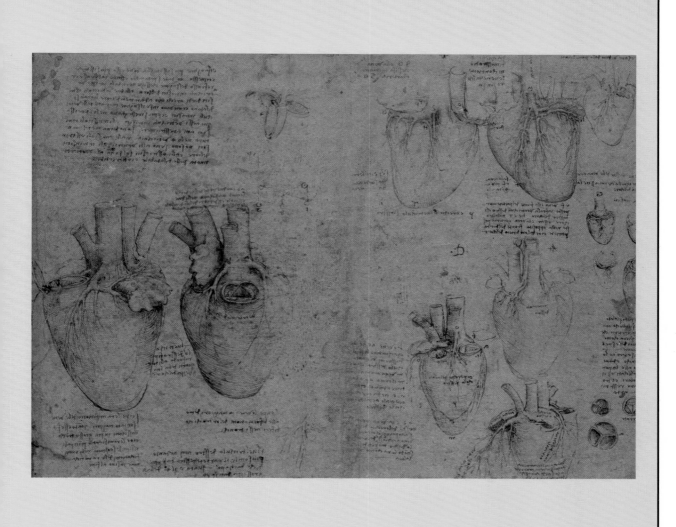

most illustrious Lord, at your much wished for restoration to health that my own malady almost left me.' When Giuliano died in March 1516, Leonardo was left lonely and neglected in Rome.

In the summer of 1516, Leonardo went with Pope Leo to Bologna. There he met the new, young French King, François I, and went with him back to France, to Amboise on the banks of the River Loire.

'No one living knows more than Leonardo', said François I, King of France and Leonardo's last patron.

Above Leonardo's drawing of
Amboise, his last home.

When Leonardo reached Amboise, he was a sick man. King François lodged him in a pleasant house called Cloux near his own castle. There, Leonardo tried to get his notebooks, recording the scientific work of a lifetime, into some kind of order.

While in Amboise, Leonardo painted a mysterious picture of the young St John. This figure seemed to have some of the features of a man and some of a woman. Many people have guessed at what Leonardo is trying to say in this painting. Perhaps this was his ideal human being, a person who has the virtues of a man and a woman at the same time.

In October 1517, an Italian cardinal, Luigi d'Aragona, saw this and other paintings in Leonardo's house at Amboise. His secretary, Antonio de Beatis, made a note of the meeting. He described Leonardo as 'over seventy' when he was only sixty-four. Leonardo probably looked older than he really was because he had had a stroke and was left with a crippled right hand.

Leonardo da Vinci as an old man. This portrait, now in a Turin museum, is thought to be a self-portrait by the artist.

Leonardo's last days were a sad re-enactment of his whole life. François admired him, called him 'a great philosopher', but bothered him with daily visits, with plans for festivals and plays, just as Ludovico Sforza had done in the far-off days in Milan. Leonardo's last entry in his notebook was touching, 'June 24, 1518

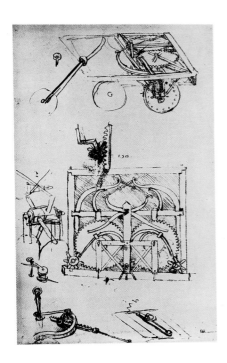

Leonardo's inventiveness was unending, but he lacked the technology which made later scientific development possible. This is his design for a mechanically powered car.

Saint John's Day at Amboise, in the palazzo of Cloux; I shall go on.' Within a year, on 2 May 1519, he was dead.

In what way was Leonardo a pioneer? Some of his ideas and inventions may seem strange to us today. But we must remember that Leonardo lived at the very beginning of the scientific age. He had no electricity, no internal combustion engine, no computers, no lasers, nor any of the technology we take for granted. More importantly, the ideas of modern science were still to be developed.

Leonardo helped to develop these ideas. He was one of the first to realize the importance of careful observation and how experiments could help the scientist. He knew that mathematics was an essential tool for the scientist. Unfortunately, Leonardo was hampered by a lack of accurate measuring instruments in his experiments. He also lacked the mathematical tools he needed.

The Scientific Revolution, in which people saw that the scientific method was the best way to study the world, began in Leonardo's time, helped along by Leonardo. One of the first fruits of this revolution was the discovery in 1543 by the Polish astronomer Nicolaus Copernicus that the Earth was not the centre of the Universe. Leonardo himself had foreseen this discovery. He saw the Earth as a 'speck in the Universe', with the Sun shining on it and other stars.

Leonardo's work on moving objects was followed up and developed by another famous Italian scientist, Galileo. In 1604, Galileo worked out exact mathematical laws to describe falling bodies. In 1687, the great English scientist, Isaac Newton, made a giant leap forward. He developed the 'laws of motion' which Leonardo had anticipated, using new mathematical methods that he had invented. Newton's laws are still the basis of all mechanical science. They represent the full flowering of the scientific revolution that started with Leonardo.

Date Chart

1452   15 April: Leonardo born in Vinci, near Florence, Italy.

1469   Starts work at workshop of Verrocchio.

1472   Admitted to the Company of Painters.

1476   Leonardo accused with others of homosexuality, but charge dismissed.

1481   Offers his services in a letter to Ludovico Sforza, ruler of Milan.

1482   Moves to Milan.

1483   Begins work on *The Virgin of the Rocks.*

1487   Starts his work on anatomy.

1492   Leonardo visits Rome. Columbus's first voyage to the New World.

1495–97   Paints the *The Last Supper.*

1499   The French invade Italy. Leonardo flees from Milan.

1500   Travels to Venice and Florence.

1501   Works on *The Virgin and Saint Anne with the Christ Child.*

1502   Employed as military engineer to Cesare Borgia.

1504   *The Battle of Anghiari* ruined. *Mona Lisa* begun.

1505   Studies flight of birds. *Mona Lisa* completed.

1506   Goes to Milan at invitation of the French King Louis XII.

1507   Returns to Florence for visit.

1508   Goes back to Milan for anatomical and other research.

1512   The French are defeated and driven from Milan.

1513   Leonardo leaves Milan and works for Giuliano de' Medici in Rome.

1516   Moves to France, to work for François I.

1519   2 May: Leonardo dies.

Books to Read

The Inventions of Leonardo da Vinci, Charles Gibbs-Smith and Gareth Rees (Phaidon, 1976)

Leonardo da Vinci and the Art of Science (Priory Press, 1977)

Leonardo the Scientist, C. Zammattio (Hutchison, 1981)

Leonardo and the Renaissance, Nick Harris (Wayland, 1980)

Glossary

Alchemy An early form of chemistry. Alchemists tried to turn iron and lead into gold, and to find a substance that would stop people growing old.

Biceps The large muscle in the front of the upper arm. The biceps bend the arm at the elbow joint.

Cartoon A preparatory drawing or sketch for copying later as a painting.

Dissect To cut up a human body or dead animal in order to study it.

Element To the Ancient Greeks, and up until the eighteenth century, an element was any of the four substances earth, air, fire and water. These were thought to be the building blocks of everything else.

Guild A union of craftsmen which kept up standards of work and protected the interests of its members.

Lever A simple machine used for lifting heavy weights, consisting of a strong bar that turns about a pivot.

Malady Sickness, illness.

Mechanics The science that studies movement and the effect of forces on an object.

Pelvis In humans and other upright animals, the bony frame at the base of the body, above the legs.

Percussion An impact or blow; described by Leonardo as the greatest of the 'four powers'.

Physics The science that studies matter, the forces of nature and the different forms of energy, such as heat, light and motion.

Renaissance The time of rediscovery and revival of ancient Greek and Roman arts and sciences. This occurred in Europe from the Middle Ages onwards to the seventeenth century. It was especially marked in Florence in the fifteenth century.

Research An investigation to discover new facts or information.

Picture acknowledgements

Bridgeman Art Library 15, 21, 31; Mary Evans cover, iii, 6, 7; Peter Newark's Western Americana 5; Quadrant Picture Library 17; Windsor Castle, Royal Library © Her Majesty The Queen 8, 32, 33, 34, 35, 36, 41, 43; The Science Museum 4, 9, 11, 12, 13, 16, 17, 18, 19 (both), 22, 23, 28, 29, 30, 37, 38, 39, 44, 45; Syndication International 42; Topham 20. Diagrams by Peter Smith. Cover artwork by Richard Hook.

Index

alchemy   37–8
Amboise   42–3
America   4
Ancient Greeks   4, 5, 40

ball-bearings   27
Battle of the Anghiari, The   30
Bologna   42
Borgia, Cesare   29

Cloux   43, 45
Copernicus   45

d'Aragona, Beatis   43
da Vinci, Leonardo
  apprenticeship   8
  attitude to women   10, 43
  birth   4, 7
  early life   7–9
  ill-health   43
  inventions   4, 10, 11–13, 14, 16–17, 27, 28, 37
  kindness to animals   10
  letter to Ludovico Sforza   12
  musical ability   13
  notebooks   22, 29, 32, 43, 44
  scientific development   6, 14, 16, 20, 22–7
  study of anatomy   8, 18, 30, 33–6, 40–41
  study of the eye   18, 20
  study of flight   16, 19, 30
  study of forces   24–7
  study of the heart   40–41
  study of light   22
  study of perspective   9, 18
  study of water   23
  theory of origins of Earth   29, 45
da Vinci, Piero   7
de' Medici, Cosimo   5
de' Medici, family   5
de' Medici, Guiliano   37–8, 40–41
de' Medici, Lorenzo   5, 10, 36
dissection   32, 40

elements   22

Ficino, Marsilio   5
Florence   4–5, 8–9, 28, 30
forces and movement   24–5, 45
fossils   29
François I, King of France   42, 44
friction   27

Galen   40
Galileo   6, 45

helicopter   16, 39

Italian states   4

Julius II, Pope   36

Last Supper, The   22
Leo X, Pope   36, 37–9, 42
Louis XII, King of France   30

maps   29
Milan   4, 14, 30, 36
Mona Lisa, The   34

Naples   4
Newton, Isaac   6, 46

Renaissance   4
Rome   4, 36, 37–41

Scientific Revolution   45
screws   39
screw-cutting machine   39
Sforza, Ludovico   11, 20, 36, 44
Sforza, Maximilian   36

Turks attack Venice   28

Venice   4, 28
Verrocchio   8–9
Vinci, village of   7
Virgin and St Anne with the Christ Child, The   29
Virgin of the Rocks, The   14